2015.

Jonathan,

You have always ma

I'm so happy your are following your passion

Love what you do in do what you love &
you'll never be working a day in you life.

Even though I'm not there everyday to
say "I love you", please know I think of
you everyday. If you ever feel down or if
im not there to talk or "text" you, pick
this book up to remember the words I want
to say in-person. Maybe someday you
can pass this onto your son. Also remember

I'm very proud of you and all of your
accomplishments. I still remember that
basketball game, when you were a kid, in
stuck to the other guy like glue!

I love you forever

Dad.

Son, even after this book is read and set aside, I hope you will remember all the wishes and thoughts it holds inside.

Copyright © 2014 by Blue Mountain Arts, Inc.

All rights reserved. No part of this publication may be reproduced, stored in a retrieval system or transmitted in any form or by any means, electronic, mechanical, photocopying, recording or otherwise, without the written permission of the publisher.

ISBN: 978-1-59842-830-8

◩ and Blue Mountain Press are registered in U.S. Patent and Trademark Office. Certain trademarks are used under license.

Printed in China.
First Printing: 2014

♻ This book is printed on recycled paper.

This book is printed on paper that has been specially produced to be acid free (neutral pH) and contains no groundwood or unbleached pulp. It conforms with the requirements of the American National Standards Institute, Inc., so as to ensure that this book will last and be enjoyed by future generations.

Blue Mountain Arts, Inc.
P.O. Box 4549, Boulder, Colorado 80306

I Want
My Son
to Know This...

Douglas Pagels

Blue Mountain Press™
Boulder, Colorado

A "forever message" for my son

Son, if there is one special message you set aside and keep forever, I hope it will be this one...

My biggest smiles come from thinking of you. My favorite memories all have reflections of you in them.

And I know how it feels to love someone with all my heart... because that's how I love you.

There are probably far too many things in my life that I take for granted. But you will never, ever be one of them. I <u>know</u> how blessed I am to have you here. In every way.

I am proud of you to the nth degree,
and I can't help thinking of what utter
and absolute joy I would have missed…
if I hadn't had the gift… of you in my life.

I would like my son to know this...

I love you so much.

I wish I could say those words to you each and every day.

I wish I could tell you how terrific you are and how grateful I will always be that I was blessed with a son like you.

And no matter how far apart we may be,
I will always be just a smile away… and
holding you close to my heart.

Son, here's some "life advice" to remember every single day

Nothing ever has and no one ever will compare with you. You deserve to be happy, to love yourself, and to be able to live your best life... every day.

Don't ever believe anyone who tells you otherwise. You matter immensely. Your wishes are so important. Your hopes and dreams are valid and valuable. And your inner strength is more powerful than you can imagine.

Never give up on the things you want to come true. Take what you want to do and need to do… and reach for it.

Life has so much to give when you hope and love and live each day in the very best way you can. There are no limits to the good you can do and the smiles you can bring to your heart.

You deserve to have so many great things come your way. One of my favorite things about being your parent is knowing — truly seeing and experiencing and appreciating — what an exceptional person you are.

I want you to see that person too. I want you to know that he is amazing and capable and able to reach just about any goal that is set.

And when it comes to a wonderful life, one that brings all the very best things to you, I want you to know how much you deserve it.

Everywhere you journey in life, you will go with my love by your side.

Forever it will be with you: truly, joyfully, and more meant to be than words could ever say.

Love is what holds
everything together.
It's the ribbon around
the gift of life.

Sharing our lives
with our loved ones
is where everything
marvelous begins.

Ask me how important my family is to me and how essential my loved ones are, and I'll tell you this simple truth... nothing else even comes close.

The incredibly special connections we have with others are the things that matter most of all.

There is nothing more wonderful than telling the ones you cherish... how much they're loved and apprcciated... every chance you get. There is no greater or more precious advice.

Love is what holds everything together. It's the ribbon around the gift of life.

No matter where you are,
a part of you will always be
here with me.

You are a treasure to my days, a smile that shines in my life, and a joy that brightens up all my hopes and dreams and memories.

I know there are lots of parents in the world, but there couldn't be a single one who is more proud of their son than I am... of you.

These are some of the gifts I want you to have...

Never forgetting how often you are in the thoughts of your loved ones.

Happiness that simply overflows... from memories made, peacefulness within, and the anticipation of so many good things to come.

Days when everything works out right
and wishing stars that come out at night
and listen to everything your heart is
hoping for.

Paths ahead that take you all the places
you want to be...

And reminders that — in so many ways —
you are such an invaluable gift, and one of
the nicest things in this entire world...
   is your presence in it.

Son, I love you so much. I want you to remember that… every single day.

I want you to know that these
are things I'll always hope and pray:

That the world will treat you fairly.

That people will appreciate the
one-in-a-million person you are.

That you will be safe and smart and
sure to make good choices on your
journey through life.

That a wealth of opportunities will come your way.

That your blessings will be many and your troubles will be few.

And that life will be very generous in giving you all the happiness and success you deserve.

Positive thoughts
to inspire your life!

Let yourself get all wrapped up in the present moment. Rest assured, it's a good place to be. Open the door to more possibilities.

Give yourself the gift of special, loving connections and the forever kind of friends.

Close the door on more worries. Have hope that never ends.

Be strong and brave and courageous.

Whenever stress has more of a place in your days than it should, find the healthiest, best, and most gratifying way to achieve more calm and serenity.

Balance things out.

Always walk with honor and integrity on the journey ahead… but don't be serious all the time. Life should be enjoyed. Have fun with it.

Listen to your heart. Open up to the prospect of a tremendously creative idea… and just run with it.

Give yourself more credit for all the amazing things you do!

Keep on reaching out, realizing that embracing life with open arms is where some of the secret joys are found. Always — always — use the golden rule as your guide.

Share a smile and get one back every single time. Make way for curiosity in your thoughts... and make a place for compassion in your heart.

Do what you can to make your corner of the world… just shine.

Remember that having a wish list is good, but having a checklist is great.

Stay the course… with an active, wholesome lifestyle, a treasure of connections, a sense of giving more than you take, and making this world a better place every chance you get.

Keep your emotional baggage carry-on size, and know that whenever a problem comes along… you can rise above it.

And since you only have one life…
live it so you'll love it.

You're not just a fantastic son. You're a tremendous, rare, and extraordinary person.

All the different facets of your life — the ones you reveal to the rest of the world and the ones known only to those you're close to — are so impressive.

And as people look even deeper, I know they can't help but see how wonderful you are inside.

I'll always love you, Son, with all my heart.

And I couldn't be more proud of you... if I tried.

I couldn't have asked for a more amazing or a more remarkable son… and I want to thank you for bringing so many smiles into my life. Thank you for being in all my favorite memories, all my highest hopes, and all my most thankful prayers.

We never know how life will turn out...
or what the years will bring. But I want
you to know this: of all the things I could
have been, I will always be grateful beyond
words... that I got to be the parent of the
best son in the whole wide world.

I got to be yours.

About the Author

Best-selling author and editor
Douglas Pagels has inspired
millions of readers with his
insights and his anthologies. His
books have sold over 3 million
copies, and he is one of the most
quoted contemporary writers on
the Internet today. Reflecting a
philosophy that is perfect for our
times, Doug has a wonderful

knack for sharing his thoughts and sentiments in a voice
that is so positive and understanding we can't help but take
the message to heart.

His writings have been translated into over a dozen
languages due to their global appeal and inspiring
outlook on life, and his work has been quoted by many
worthy causes and charitable organizations.

He and his wife live in Colorado, and they are the
parents of children in college and beyond. Over the
years, Doug has spent much of his time as a classroom
volunteer, a youth basketball coach, an advocate for
local environmental issues, a frequent traveler, and a
craftsman, building a cabin in the Rocky Mountains.